Original title:
Joyful Journey

Copyright © 2024 Creative Arts Management OÜ
All rights reserved.

Author: Thor Castlebury
ISBN HARDBACK: 978-9916-88-234-4
ISBN PAPERBACK: 978-9916-88-235-1

Horizons Bright with Dreams

Beyond the hills where skies embrace,
Whispers of hope in a gentle space.
Colors dance in the morning light,
Awakening visions, bold and bright.

As shadows fade with the rising sun,
New paths unfold, adventures begun.
Chasing the echoes of laughter's grace,
In the embrace of time's sweet trace.

Cups Overflowing with Sunshine

A cup brimming with joyous cheer,
Sweet warmth that draws loved ones near.
Laughter spills like golden wine,
Moments savored, hearts entwine.

In every sip, memories bloom,
Chasing away the lingering gloom.
With every toast, the world shines bright,
A celebration of pure delight.

Flights of Fancy

In dreams we soar on wings of light,
To places where the heart feels right.
Clouds like castles, skies aglow,
Adventures waiting, time to flow.

Imagination paints the skies,
With colors bold, where magic lies.
Each fleeting thought, a bird in flight,
Carrying hopes into the night.

Horizon's Heartbeat

Where earth meets sky, a pulse begins,
An endless rhythm that softly spins.
With every wave that kisses shore,
A whisper of dreams and so much more.

As day breaks forth, the canvas spreads,
With varying hues of golden threads.
In every heartbeat, nature sings,
A timeless dance that hope forever brings.

The Melody of Miles

With each step, a story grows,
Echoes of laughter in whispered flows.
Footprints linger on winding trails,
In the heart of travel, a spirit prevails.

Rhythms of life in each journey found,
The world sings softly, a beautiful sound.
Mountains watch over dreams that rise,
Underneath ever-changing skies.

Exploring Elysium

In fields where wildflowers sway,
Golden sun greets the dawning day.
Wings of freedom touch the ground,
In this paradise, peace is found.

Whispers of breezes through the trees,
Moments captured, carried by the seas.
Starlit nights that dance above,
In the land of dreams, we find our love.

Tracks of Delight

Along the river, shadows play,
In the warmth of a golden ray.
Tiny paths where footsteps blend,
With nature's song, our hearts ascend.

The laughter of children fills the air,
Each moment cherished, beyond compare.
Joyful echoes in laughter's wake,
On this journey, memories awake.

A Tapestry of Moments

Threads of time weave memories bright,
Each stitch a tale, a guiding light.
Colors swirl in vibrant grace,
A tapestry of moments, woven space.

Captured whispers of love and glee,
In every corner, a memory.
From laughter's spark to silent tears,
A masterpiece crafted through the years.

The Road of Radiance

Along the winding path we tread,
With sunlight glinting overhead.
The warmth of hope in every stride,
A journey blessed, with love as guide.

Through forests deep and valleys wide,
We carry dreams that won't subside.
Each step illuminated bright,
A testament to inner light.

The whispers of the leaves surround,
In nature's voice our peace is found.
Each turn reveals a new surprise,
In every heart, true wonder lies.

A Tapestry of Triumphs

In threads of gold and colors bold,
Stories of courage and dreams unfold.
Each stitch a testament to grace,
In every heart, a sacred place.

With every battle bravely fought,
Lessons learned and wisdom sought.
We weave a tale both rich and rare,
With every triumph, hearts laid bare.

Through trials faced and fears embraced,
A tapestry of life well-paced.
The beauty lies in every scar,
A journey shared, no matter how far.

Festivities of the Heart

With laughter ringing through the air,
We dance and twirl without a care.
In every smile and joyous cheer,
The spirit of love draws us near.

Through candlelight and twinkling stars,
We gather close, no matter the scars.
Connections made, and bonds we share,
In the festivities, we lay our hearts bare.

With every toast and song we sing,
A celebration of life we bring.
Moments cherished, memories bright,
In the warmth of love, we find our light.

Sails of Serenity

Upon the waves, our vessel glides,
With gentle winds as faithful guides.
Each ripple whispers peace and calm,
In nature's embrace, we find our balm.

The horizon stretches wide and free,
With sails unfurled, we feel the sea.
In tranquil waters, hearts take flight,
A journey shared under soft moonlight.

Through storms we've faced and skies so clear,
Together always, there's naught to fear.
We navigate with love as our map,
On sails of serenity, we take a nap.

Pure Bliss in Every Moment

In a sunlit glade, I pause and breathe,
Nature's whispers are a gentle weave.
Every ray touches my heart anew,
Finding joy in all that I pursue.

Soft breezes dance through the emerald leaves,
A moment like this, my spirit believes.
Time stands still, in a blissful trance,
Life unfolds in a lovely romance.

Steps Beneath the Stars

Under a vaulted sky, we walk and dream,
Stars twinkle above, a shimmering gleam.
With every step, the night softly sings,
Whispers of hope, on delicate wings.

Hand in hand, we trace the cosmos high,
In the stillness, our worries fly.
Each step we take, a universe found,
In the vastness, our love does abound.

Pathways of Delight

Through winding trails, where flowers bloom,
Each path we take dispels all gloom.
Laughter echoes, as we wander wide,
Together forever, side by side.

Sunlight dances on the afternoon,
Joyful heartbeats keep perfect tune.
Every turn reveals a new surprise,
Magic explored, under azure skies.

Treasuring the Travels

Miles and memories, closely entwined,
Every journey leaves a mark in kind.
With each new place, another tale spun,
In the fabric of life, we are one.

Starlit skies and oceans deep,
Treasured moments, forever we keep.
In the heart, the wanderlust stays,
Guiding our steps through endless days.

A Journey to Remember

Through valleys and mountains we roam,
Each step a memory, far from home.
We laugh and we learn, hand in hand,
Together we wander, across this land.

The sunsets paint skies in fiery hues,
While stardust whispers our favorite tunes.
With hearts wide open, we chase the light,
Creating our story, both bold and bright.

Sweet Whimsy of Wandering

In the meadows where wildflowers sway,
We dance with the breeze, come what may.
Butterflies flutter, our spirits take flight,
The world feels alive beneath the soft light.

With every twist, another surprise,
A treasure awaits beneath open skies.
We find joy in the simplest things,
As laughter and love become our wings.

Radiance in Every Step

Each footprint we leave, a mark of our way,
Illuminated paths where our dreams can play.
With hope in our hearts and the stars as our guide,
We move through the shadows, never to hide.

The sun arches high, painting gold on the near,
In the stillness of morning, our vision is clear.
So we walk hand in hand, through laughter and tears,
Finding strength in our love that only grows near.

Whispers of Happiness

In the silence of night, secrets unfold,
Stories of joy and love yet untold.
Moonlit reflections dance on the stream,
Awakening hearts, igniting a dream.

With every soft breeze that brushes our skin,
Whispers of happiness beckon within.
We raise up our voices, a beautiful song,
Together in harmony, where we belong.

Harvesting Sunshine

Golden rays upon the field,
Nature's bounty, gently healed.
Whispers of the wind's embrace,
Harvest time, a joyful chase.

Fingers brushing golden grain,
In the warmth, we feel no pain.
Laughter echoes, hearts align,
As we gather, sun will shine.

Ripened fruits, the trees bow low,
Gifts of earth in vibrant glow.
Every heartbeat, gratitude,
In this moment, love renewed.

As the day begins to fade,
Memories of sun's parade.
Hope and peace in every bite,
Harvesting through day and night.

The Way of Gladness

In the morning's gentle light,
Joy awakens, pure and bright.
With each step, the world unfolds,
Stories waiting to be told.

Laughter dances on the breeze,
Carried far through ancient trees.
Heart and soul in harmony,
Living life so willingly.

Every glance, a spark of glee,
Kindred spirits, you and me.
Joyful hearts in every stride,
In this journey, we confide.

Even shadows may descend,
Love and hope will always mend.
In the evening's soft embrace,
We'll find gladness in this place.

Whimsical Wanderings

Beneath the sky of endless dreams,
We follow paths where sunlight beams.
Whispers of adventure call,
In each moment, we stand tall.

Through meadows bright and forests deep,
With every step, our spirits leap.
Curious hearts, we roam and play,
Finding magic in the day.

Clouds like cotton, drifting slow,
Painted skies, a vibrant show.
Hand in hand, we chase the light,
Savoring the world in flight.

Every turn, a tale to tell,
In the secrets hidden well.
Whimsical, our hearts aligned,
In our wanderings, joy we find.

Summit of Serenity

Above the chaos, skies so clear,
In the stillness, we draw near.
Mountains rise, their peaks in grace,
A tranquil heart, a sacred space.

Breath of nature, pure and sweet,
In stillness, all our worries meet.
With every moment, calm descends,
On this path, the soul transcends.

Clouds below, like dreams that soar,
Here on high, we seek for more.
Silent whispers, peace inside,
In this summit, love abides.

As the sun begins to set,
Moments linger, never fret.
In this haven, nature's key,
We find solace, you and me.

A Mosaic of Mirth

In the garden where laughter blooms,
Colors dance in vibrant rooms.
Joy spills like sunlight through the trees,
Whispers of happiness in the breeze.

Each smile a piece, so brightly laid,
Crafting a tapestry, hand-made.
Together we laugh, we sing, we play,
Creating our world in a colorful way.

Under the sky, so wide and blue,
Mirrors of joy reflect in dew.
Every heartbeats a note in the song,
United in mirth, where we all belong.

Let's dance in the rain, let worries cease,
In this mosaic, we find our peace.
Hand in hand, let the good times start,
A canvas of laughter painted from the heart.

The Journey of Gleeful Hearts

We set forth with spirits high,
A path of joy beneath the sky.
Footsteps light, our laughter shared,
With glances sweet, our hearts are bared.

Through the valleys, over hills,
Chasing dreams, excitement thrills.
In every moment, pure delight,
Together we make the dark seem bright.

Stars adorn our evening stroll,
In every smile, we find our goal.
Winding roads lead us anew,
With gleeful hearts, we break on through.

At each bend, new wonders gleam,
Kindred souls in a joyful dream.
The journey's magic, a treasure vast,
In every heartbeat, love is cast.

Boundless Horizons of Happiness

On the shores of endless bliss,
Where every moment starts with a kiss.
The waves of joy crash on the sand,
Embracing life, hand in hand.

Underneath the golden sun,
Endless laughter just begun.
With every sunrise, hopes arise,
Painting the world in vibrant skies.

Exploring realms where dreams take flight,
Chasing stars that shimmer bright.
Each turn we take leads us to a scene,
Where happiness reigns, serene and keen.

In the vastness, our spirits soar,
Finding treasures forevermore.
Boundless horizons whispering sweet,
In this journey, our hearts repeat.

Sojourns with a Smile

With every step, we roam so free,
In lands of joy, just you and me.
Smiles greet us at every door,
In sojourns that we can't ignore.

Through meadows bright, we chase the light,
Every moment feels so right.
The laughter echoes through the air,
In simple things, love is laid bare.

Mountains high and rivers wide,
We journey forth, side by side.
In whispers shared, our hearts entwine,
Finding magic in the divine.

As the sun sets with a golden hue,
We count the blessings, me and you.
Together we weave, wherever we roam,
In sojourns with smiles, we find our home.

Festive Journeys

Colors blaze in the night,
Joy dances in the air.
Laughter echoes, hearts alight,
Every moment, a delightful flare.

Hands held tight, we roam,
Under canopies of stars.
The world feels just like home,
As we travel beyond the bars.

Delicious scents waft near,
From stalls lined in cheer.
Sharing smiles, we draw near,
Memories woven, crystal clear.

With every step, new friends greet,
A tapestry of love we weave.
In this festive, joyous feat,
Together, we will always believe.

Revelations on the Path

Whispers of the trees so wise,
Secrets linger in the breeze.
Each step unveils the skies,
While the heart learns to seize.

Footprints mark our journey's trace,
Every turn, a new embrace.
Lessons bloom in nature's grace,
Guiding us through this timeless space.

Stars above gleam with intent,
Mirroring dreams we send.
Eager minds, our thoughts relent,
To discoveries that never end.

In silence, truths arise,
Holding beauty in their hand.
On this road, wisdom lies,
Inviting us to understand.

An Unexpected Adventure

Beneath a sky of endless gray,
A twist of fate calls me near.
An unplanned path, I can't delay,
With the unknown, I'll break my fear.

Torn maps lie scattered around,
But the thrill ignites my soul.
In every lost place, magic is found,
As I wander, learning to stroll.

Chasing shadows and sunlight beams,
My heart races with delight.
In this dance of wild dreams,
I embrace each turn and flight.

A friendly face, a guiding hand,
In laughter, we share the ride.
Together, discovering this land,
With every moment, dreams collide.

Radiant Days Ahead

Morning dew glistens bright,
Awakening the world anew.
With each sunrise, golden light,
Paints our dreams in vibrant hue.

Paths we wander, side by side,
Filled with hopes of a clear sky.
Hand in hand, we shall abide,
Chasing moments that will fly.

Laughter sparkles in the air,
Promises of joy yet to unfold.
With an open heart, we dare,
To welcome stories yet untold.

Radiant days are ours to find,
In the journey that we share.
Leaving yesterday behind,
With love lighting every care.

The Art of Playful Exploration

In fields of dreams we run and twirl,
With laughter echoing, our spirits unfurl.
Every shadow holds a secret to find,
A treasure chest of wonders, unconfined.

We chase the breeze and dance with light,
In every corner, magic ignites.
With open hearts, we wander the scene,
Where joy resides, wild and serene.

Roads Less Traveled

Through forest paths and rivers deep,
Where whispers of the ancient seep.
With every turn, the world expands,
As nature's wonders take our hands.

The cliffs may call, the valleys sing,
In quiet corners, inspiration springs.
With footsteps light, we find our way,
In hidden realms where dreams can play.

Sun-kissed Pathways

Beneath the sun, the flowers bloom,
Each petal weaving nature's loom.
A golden trail winds through the green,
With every step, a love unseen.

The warmth envelops, soft and bright,
As clouds drift by, in dance and flight.
With arms outstretched to the warm embrace,
We lose ourselves in this sacred space.

Explorations in Exuberance

Our laughter fills the air like song,
In every heartbeat, we belong.
With courage bold, we leap and dive,
In wild adventures, we come alive.

The world is vast, horizons wide,
With magic waiting deep inside.
Hand in hand, we traverse the night,
In playful spirit, we find our light.

Dancing Through Sunlit Paths

Amidst the trees, we twirl and sway,
Bright beams of gold lead us on our way.
With each soft step, our spirits rise,
Hand in hand, beneath the skies.

Laughter echoes, a joyful sound,
As nature's peace wraps around.
We chase the light, in gentle grace,
In this moment, we find our place.

The whispers of leaves, a soft refrain,
We dance through sunshine, through gentle rain.
With every heartbeat, we feel the cheer,
Together we spin, with nothing to fear.

As twilight falls, our shadows blend,
In this sunlit path, we find no end.
With memories made, in each embrace,
We dance through life, at our own pace.

Embrace of the Unseen Breeze

A whisper soft, a gentle touch,
The unseen breeze, it means so much.
It dances past, through every hair,
A tender gift, beyond all care.

In fields of green, the wildflowers sway,
Embraced by air, they find their way.
With every shift, it sings a song,
Inviting hearts to dance along.

The rustling leaves, they start to laugh,
In nature's arms, we feel its path.
With eyes closed tight, we breathe it in,
An unseen force, where dreams begin.

So let us sway, like branches high,
In the embrace of the sky.
In every moment, let's drift and roam,
With the unseen breeze, we find our home.

A Canvas Painted with Laughter

Brush strokes of joy, colors bright,
On a canvas filled with light.
Each laugh sets free, a vibrant hue,
Painting a world, both fresh and new.

In every smile, a story lives,
A tapestry, the heart gives.
The joy we share, spreads like flame,
In this artwork, we find our name.

From blues of calm to reds of cheer,
Our laughter echoes, loud and clear.
Together we blend, creating bliss,
In every moment, in every kiss.

So let us color outside the lines,
In this canvas, our love shines.
With laughter bright, let's paint and play,
A masterpiece for every day.

Steps of Delight

With every step, a new surprise,
A dance begins beneath the skies.
In fields of dreams, we wander free,
Each moment shared, just you and me.

The path unfolds, a joyful call,
Together we rise, we'll never fall.
With hearts aligned, we skip and twirl,
In this world, let our dreams unfurl.

Through grassy knolls and sunny lanes,
We weave our tales with no restraints.
With every giggle, our spirits soar,
In steps of delight, we ask for more.

So take my hand, let's run and play,
In this life, we'll find our way.
With steps of delight, our souls take flight,
Together forever, shining bright.

Into the Garden of Wonders

Beneath the arch of verdant leaves,
A whisper trails the morning breeze.
Petals blush with colors bright,
As soft sunbeams dance in light.

In hidden nooks where secrets dwell,
The blooming scents cast a sweet spell.
Every corner holds delight,
Inviting hearts to take flight.

A symphony of buzzing bees,
In harmony with swaying trees.
Paths of magic, winding slow,
Lead us where the wildflowers grow.

Yet as the twilight starts to fade,
The garden weaves a twilight shade.
In starlit silence, dreams arise,
Awakening the night's surprise.

The Odyssey of Cheer

Upon the waves of laughter bright,
We sail through days, a joyful flight.
Each moment shines, a treasure trove,
In every heart, our spirits rove.

The sun bestows its golden gleam,
In playful glances, we all dream.
From dawn to dusk, we weave our song,
With memories that linger long.

Through storms we dance, with hope so clear,
Our journey blessed, forever near.
With every step, we chase the light,
In this odyssey of pure delight.

Bound by bonds that never sever,
In every heart, we find forever.
So let us cheer, with voices strong,
Together we belong, we belong.

Echoes of Bliss

In whispered winds, the echoes play,
Soft melodies of a sunny day.
Each note a dance, a fleeting chance,
To savor life in a joyous trance.

With laughter ringing through the air,
Moments cherished, tender and rare.
A gentle call from days gone by,
In echoes soft as a lullaby.

Through fields of dreams, we wander free,
In every heart, a symphony.
Let love's embrace weave through the mist,
And guide us to the moments kissed.

For in the stillness, joy remains,
In every sorrow, bliss contains.
So heed the echoes, let them flow,
In every heart, let happiness grow.

Festive Footprints

Beneath the stars, the laughter rings,
As joy ignites in cheerful flings.
With every step, the night awakes,
In festive souls, the spirit breaks.

Candles glow with warmth and cheer,
Inviting all to gather near.
The sound of music fills the air,
As happiness is shared everywhere.

From corner to corner, smiles abound,
In every heart, a rhythm found.
The night's embrace, a joyful dance,
In festive footprints, we take our chance.

So let us cherish every sound,
In memories and moments profound.
With dreams ignited under the moon,
Together here, our hearts attune.

Trails of Euphoria

In fields of gold, we dance and play,
Chasing sunlight through the day.
Each step a joy, each breath a sigh,
As laughter lifts us toward the sky.

With hearts unbound, we wander free,
Through fragrant blooms, beneath the trees.
The trails we walk, a blissful song,
In moments fleeting, we belong.

The whispering winds share secrets sweet,
As twilight beckons, our souls compete.
For joy is found in every turn,
A spark ignites, a fire to burn.

So hold my hand and run with me,
On trails of love, where we can be.
In every smile, our spirits soar,
Together, we will seek for more.

Whirlwinds of Whimsy

Around we spin, in sudden bursts,
With laughter light that never hurts.
The world a canvas, wild and bright,
With colors dancing in pure delight.

We chase the clouds above the trees,
Laughing loud on the playful breeze.
Each day a journey, a brand-new game,
In whirlwinds of joy, we stake our claim.

Through twists and turns, we weave our dreams,
In fantastical realms, where sunlight beams.
A sprinkle of magic in every sway,
As whimsy leads us, we gladly play.

So let us twirl, let us rejoice,
In this great dance, we find our voice.
Together, we ignite the fun,
In whirlwinds of whimsy, we are one.

The Landscape of Laughter

Amidst the hills where shadows fall,
We gather round, a joyful thrall.
With every chuckle, we paint the air,
In a landscape brimming with love and care.

The paths we tread, a treasure map,
Each giggle shared, a gentle clap.
As echoes rise, our spirits gleam,
In this vast land, we dare to dream.

Under the stars, with stories spun,
We weave our tales, our hearts in one.
The moonlight adds a silver hue,
To moments bright and laughter true.

So let us roam this joyous land,
With open hearts and dreams so grand.
For in laughter's glow, we shall find,
The landscape of joy, forever aligned.

Bubbles Floating on the Wind

Delicate spheres, they drift away,
Catching sunlight in soft ballet.
With colors swirling, they break the mold,
A dance of dreams, both pure and bold.

They rise and fall, in playful spirals,
Floating free, like sweet revival.
In moments fleeting, they tease the eye,
A wish upon each, as they pass by.

With every pop, a dream takes flight,
Under the stars, in the quiet night.
These bubbles sing of hopes anew,
In whispers soft, their essence true.

So let us chase what's light and bright,
With hearts like bubbles, in joyful flight.
For in their glow, we come to see,
The magic found in being free.

The Lightness of Being

In the whisper of dawn's embrace,
A dance of shadows leaves no trace.
With every breath, the world feels free,
The lightness of being, just to be.

Clouds drift softly, a gentle sigh,
As dreams are woven in the sky.
Moments lift like petals in flight,
In this soft world, all feels right.

The heart knows joy without the weight,
In laughter shared, it learns to wait.
Each fleeting gaze, a spark ignites,
An echo of love in simple sights.

Together we dance, hand in hand,
In this lightness, we take a stand.
With open hearts, we learn to see,
The essence of being, wild and free.

Journey's End as a Beginning

The road winds on, its twists and bends,
Each step a tale, where time transcends.
With weary feet and hearts so bold,
We find new paths in stories told.

When hours fade and daylight wanes,
A whisper calls beyond the plains.
In every end, a spark alights,
A journey's end, new dawn ignites.

The echoes of laughter, memories clear,
Guide us home, as we draw near.
With open arms, we greet the change,
In every heart, life must rearrange.

So let us step where shadows blend,
For every journey starts again.
In every goodbye, a promise glows,
A journey's end, as life bestows.

Explorations in Every Smile

In every smile, a story hides,
A world of wonders gently bides.
Eyes that twinkle, a spark so bright,
Explorations bloom in pure delight.

From strangers met on winding streets,
Connections formed in moments sweet.
In laughter shared, our spirits grow,
In the simplest things, love's river flows.

The warmth of kindness, a soft embrace,
In every smile, we find our place.
With hearts wide open, we learn to share,
In every smile, the world is fair.

So let us cherish, each fleeting glance,
In every smile, we find our chance.
To weave a tapestry, life's gentle thread,
Explorations bloom, where love has led.

Adventures in Awakening

In the quiet dawn of day,
New horizons call my name,
With every step, I find my way,
Life's a dance, a joyful game.

Colors burst in morning light,
Each moment whispers and sings,
Awakening my heart so bright,
To embrace what each day brings.

Chasing dreams through fields of gold,
With every breath, the world expands,
In stories new and tales retold,
I find my place in life's vast plans.

Together with the rising sun,
With hope and faith that never fades,
Adventures start, and I will run,
Through paths of light where joy cascades.

The Embrace of Every Moment

In the stillness of the night,
Stars are scattered, dreams take flight,
Moments pass, yet here I stay,
In gentle waves of time's ballet.

Awareness blooms in simple things,
A child's laugh, a bird that sings,
The embrace of now, a sacred space,
In each heartbeat, find my grace.

Seasons shift, the world will change,
Yet in stillness, I'm not estranged,
Each fleeting second, pure and bright,
Holds the magic of our sight.

With open eyes, I walk the road,
Finding joy in every load,
For life unfolds, a canvas vast,
In each moment, love is cast.

A Wondrous Expedition

With a heart so full of dreams,
I venture forth where sunlight beams,
Mountains rise and rivers flow,
Adventure calls, I'm ready to go.

Through forests deep and valleys wide,
Nature's wonders, my trusty guide,
Every leaf, and stone, and breeze,
Whispers secrets among the trees.

Paths may twist and skies may gray,
Yet hope's a fire that lights the way,
In each challenge, strength I find,
A wondrous journey for the mind.

Together we shall seek and roam,
With every step, we carve our home,
For in this world, both vast and bright,
Lies the thrill of the unknown night.

Heartbeats in Harmony

In the rhythm of life's embrace,
Two hearts dance in shared space,
Every beat, a whispered rhyme,
Creating melodies through time.

As moonlight bathes the sleeping night,
Our love ignites, a glowing light,
In perfect sync, we find our song,
Together where we both belong.

Moments woven, soft and tight,
In laughter shared and dreams in flight,
With every sigh, our spirits soar,
In harmony forevermore.

Through trials faced and joys we claim,
Our love's the spark, the cherished flame,
In this dance of life, we partake,
Heartbeats united, never break.

Celebrating the Present

In the sun's warm glow we gather,
Laughter dances in the air,
Moments wrapped in golden thread,
Cherishing now without a care.

Time stands still in joyful hearts,
Each breath a gift, a treasure true,
Together we weave memories bright,
In this moment, me and you.

Eyes sparkling with dreams untold,
Future waits, but here we dwell,
Basking in this truth unfolding,
In the present, all is well.

Let the music play on loud,
As we toast to life so sweet,
Celebrating all that we are,
Every heartbeat, every beat.

Trails of Triumph

Up the mountain, paths are steep,
Yet we rise, with spirits bold,
Each step a story we will keep,
In the journey, new and old.

Through the valleys, shadows cast,
Light breaks forth with every stride,
Turning trials into triumphs,
With the strength we find inside.

Every bend reveals a view,
Nature's canvas, vibrant, grand,
We march on, our goal in sight,
Hand in hand, we'll make our stand.

With each summit, we will cheer,
For the battles fought with grace,
Trails of triumph, year by year,
In our hearts, we find our place.

Savoring the Scenic

Over hills and valleys green,
Nature whispers soft and low,
Colors blend in perfect scene,
Where the gentle breezes blow.

In the wild where rivers run,
We pause to breathe the fragrant air,
Every moment, pure and fun,
Savoring all that we can share.

Mountains high, and oceans wide,
Capture beauty, touch the soul,
Wanderlust we cannot hide,
In each landscape, we feel whole.

Sunset's glow, a work of art,
As day whispers its sweet goodbye,
Together we will roam and chart,
The scenic world's endless sky.

Exultation in Every Step

With each footfall, feel the ground,
Heartbeat rising with the song,
In this rhythm, joy is found,
Moving forward, bold and strong.

Through the forest, on the trail,
Nature calls with vibrant cheer,
Every whisper, every tale,
Echoes bright for us to hear.

Celebrating life's great dance,
Every moment, pure delight,
Seize the day, take each chance,
In the shadows, find the light.

Exultation fills the air,
As we journey side by side,
In our hearts, a love so rare,
In every step, our hopes reside.

Laughter in the Breeze

Laughter dances on the air,
Carried softly everywhere.
Whispers of joy, so light and free,
Mingle with the rustling tree.

Sunshine glows in golden hues,
Painting skies with vibrant views.
Children's giggles fill the park,
Innocence ignites the spark.

A gentle breeze begins to sway,
Carrying worries far away.
Every chuckle, every cheer,
Brings the world a little near.

Hearts unite in pure delight,
Laughter echoes day and night.
In this moment, joy's increase,
Life unfolds, a sweet release.

Horizons of Happiness

Across the hills, the sun will rise,
Painting dreams across the skies.
Laughter waits at every turn,
In each heart, a flame will burn.

Footsteps on this vibrant land,
With hope and love, we take our stand.
Together, we can face the dawn,
In our unity, fears are gone.

Waves of joy, they crash and flow,
In the warmth, our spirits grow.
Every moment, rich and bright,
Guides us gently to the light.

Horizons stretch, both wide and far,
In this galaxy, you are the star.
Embrace the journey, cherish it true,
Horizons of happiness, made for you.

Beneath the Starlit Sky

Beneath the stars, we share our dreams,
In whispered tales, the night redeems.
Moonlit paths of silver glow,
Guiding hearts where love can grow.

Each twinkling light tells a story,
Of distant worlds and fleeting glory.
In the stillness, peace unfolds,
Magic dances, dreams retold.

The night air hums a gentle tune,
Crickets chirp beneath the moon.
With every breath, the cosmos sings,
In this embrace, our spirit clings.

Together here, we feel so free,
Infinite as the endless sea.
Beneath the stars, hearts combined,
In the universe, we're entwined.

Wings of Whimsy

On wings of whimsy, we take flight,
To lands where colors feel so bright.
Each flutter brings a vibrant sound,
Where laughter's joy is always found.

Frolic through fields of wildflowers,
Time stands still for endless hours.
Creativity blooms in the air,
In this realm, we're free from care.

Magic swirls around the bend,
Every moment, a joyful blend.
With every step, our spirits soar,
Exploring realms we've yet to explore.

Together we weave a tapestry,
Of dreams and hopes, of you and me.
On wings of whimsy, side by side,
In this adventure, let's abide.

The Heart's Expedition

In the quiet of the night,
Whispers guide the soul's flight.
Every dream, a star to chase,
In love's arms, we find our place.

Mountains rise, and rivers flow,
With each step, the feelings grow.
Through the valleys, the journey's long,
The heart beats, a steadfast song.

In the shadows, fears may hide,
But together, we turn the tide.
Hand in hand, we face the storm,
In every trial, our hearts grow warm.

Through the skies, we seek the light,
In the dark, we find our might.
This expedition, a tale of trust,
For love's compass, we shall adjust.

Sunbeams on Winding Trails

Golden rays through trees peek,
On the path, the whispers speak.
Each step dances with delight,
Nature's canvas, pure and bright.

Winding trails, where shadows play,
Silent laughter leads the way.
In the breeze, a soft embrace,
Every turn unveils a grace.

Flowers bloom along the way,
Painting dreams in colors gay.
In sunbeams, our spirits soar,
Finding joy in every core.

With each inch, new wonders grow,
Through the heart, the rivers flow.
In these moments, we prevail,
Together, on these winding trails.

Serendipity's Embrace

In chance encounters, smiles ignite,
Fate's own hand, a wondrous sight.
Moments woven, threads so fine,
In serendipity, we intertwine.

A glance exchanged, hearts collide,
In the mist, where dreams reside.
Unexpected paths become our guide,
In the dance where love won't hide.

With every laugh, the world expands,
In the magic of life's demands.
A simple touch, a gentle grace,
In serendipity's warm embrace.

Destinies align with ease,
In the whispers of the trees.
Every heartbeat's a sweet refrain,
In the joys of love's own gain.

A Symphony of Smiles

In a world where laughter sings,
Joyful notes on gentle wings.
A symphony of radiant beams,
Filling hearts with vibrant dreams.

Each smile shared, a melody,
Weaving tales of harmony.
Through the ups and through the downs,
Life's sweet music drapes the crowns.

With every laugh, the spirit gleams,
Creating light from whispered themes.
Together in this joyful race,
A symphony of smiles we trace.

As the chorus starts to rise,
Hope is found within our ties.
In life's dance, we find our roles,
A symphony that heals our souls.

Embracing the Unexpected

In the stillness of the night,
Dreams take flight, chasing light.
Paths diverge, often unclear,
Yet in uncertainty, we steer.

Moments change with every breath,
Whispers of fate dance with death.
Beyond the plan, a wild call,
In chaos, we can rise or fall.

Through shadows, the heart may race,
Finding joy in the unknown space.
Life unfolds like a book unturned,
Each page a lesson, brightly burned.

With open arms, we greet the strange,
From fear, we learn to redefine change.
Embrace the twists, the turns we take,
In the unexpected, our spirits awake.

Radiance on the Road

The path ahead is lit with gold,
Every step a story told.
Through valleys deep and mountains high,
A treasure waits beneath the sky.

Footprints trailing, memories vast,
With every mile, we shed the past.
Moments shine like stars at night,
Guided by hope and pure delight.

In the distance, horizons gleam,
Carrying the warmth of a dream.
The journey winds, but hearts stay bold,
Each detour reveals wonders untold.

Together we traverse the dawn,
With love that binds and won't be gone.
Radiance shines on this road we roam,
In every footstep, we build our home.

Kaleidoscope of Colors

A world awash in vibrant hues,
Each shade a story, old and new.
Petals dance in the gentle breeze,
Nature's palette, sure to please.

From golden sun to emerald grass,
Every color, a moment to grasp.
The ocean's deep, a sapphire glow,
In every wave, the colors flow.

Life unfolds in a vivid dream,
With every glance, we share the scheme.
A tapestry of joy and pain,
In every stitch, we break the chain.

Beneath the sky's vast, painted dome,
We find the hues that lead us home.
In this kaleidoscope, hearts ignite,
Together we shine, a radiant light.

Serendipity's Embrace

A chance encounter, a fleeting glance,
In the chaos, a hidden dance.
Life unfolds in curious ways,
Woven through unexpected days.

Moments align, like stars above,
In the quiet, we find our love.
Serendipity sings her song,
In the right place, we all belong.

Paths cross like rivers flow,
Bringing warmth during the snow.
Each twist and turn a gift to treasure,
In small surprises, we find our measure.

So here's to fate and all it brings,
In the dance of life, our spirit sings.
Embrace the flow, let worries cease,
In serendipity, we find our peace.

Glistening Moments

Soft whispers of the night fall,
Stars twinkle, echoing a call.
Every heartbeat sings in tune,
Dancing softly beneath the moon.

Flashes of laughter fill the air,
Memories made without a care.
Time slows down, a gentle breeze,
In glistening moments, hearts find ease.

The warmth of friendship lights the way,
Guiding us through night and day.
Together we savor every bliss,
In these moments, life's pure kiss.

As dawn approaches, colors blend,
With glistening moments that won't end.
Hold them close, let spirits soar,
In each heartbeat, we find more.

A Quest for Delight

Across the hills we chase the light,
In every shadow, there's delight.
With open hearts, we wander free,
In nature's arms, we long to be.

The laughter of children fills the air,
As dreams unfold without a care.
Each step we take, a chance to see,
The wonders that life offers, endlessly.

Through winding paths and hidden trails,
We find joy where the spirit hails.
In every smile, a spark ignites,
A quest for delight, our hearts take flight.

Embracing moments, fleeting yet bright,
We gather memories, pure and light.
With every sunset painting the sky,
Our quest for delight will never die.

Dancing Through the Kaleidoscope

Colors swirl in vibrant streams,
Life unfolds like whispered dreams.
We twirl beneath the painted skies,
In a world where wonder lies.

Each twist reveals a new delight,
A symphony of day and night.
Faces change, yet joy remains,
In the dance, there are no chains.

Through patterns of the heart we glide,
In kaleidoscopic love, we bide.
A moment captured, down we sway,
Dancing ever, come what may.

With open arms, we embrace time,
In this rhythm, all feels sublime.
Together we'll spin and play,
In the kaleidoscope, forever stay.

The Pursuit of Bliss

With every step, the heart takes flight,
In the pursuit of joy, pure and bright.
Chasing dreams across the sky,
With every laugh, we learn to fly.

In sunlit gardens, we find our peace,
Where worries fade and sorrows cease.
Hand in hand, we wander far,
In the pursuit of bliss, we are a star.

Through valleys deep and mountains high,
We seek the truth, we seek the sky.
In every moment, love's embrace,
Brings us closer to that sacred place.

As twilight hues begin to blend,
The journey never seems to end.
With open hearts, we shall persist,
In the pursuit of our sweetest bliss.

Splendid Sojourns

Beneath a sky of azure bright,
We wander paths that spark delight.
Each step reveals a world anew,
With every turn, the dreams pursue.

Golden fields where wildflowers dance,
In whispers soft, they weave romance.
Mountains rise in stately grace,
Inviting us to join the chase.

Rivers sing in gentle flow,
Their melodies, a tale to know.
Through wooded trails and valleys wide,
Nature's canvas, our hearts abide.

As sun dips low, the stars ignite,
In splendid sojourns, we take flight.
Together, we embrace the night,
In dreams, we journey, hearts alight.

Echoes of Euphoria

In laughter's wake, the echoes play,
A symphony that lights the day.
With every smile, the world expands,
In joy's embrace, we take our stands.

When shadows fall, our spirits rise,
We chase the sun, we touch the skies.
Each moment shared, a treasure pure,
In echoes of euphoria, we're sure.

Beneath the moon's enchanting glow,
The heart's the compass when we go.
In rhythm of the stars above,
We find our way, we feel the love.

So let us dance, let laughter ring,
In every breath, new hope we bring.
Together, through the highs and lows,
In echoes sweet, the love still grows.

Pictures in Motion

Frames of life and love unfold,
Captured stories, vivid and bold.
In each picture, a moment held,
A tale of the heart, beautifully spelled.

Through lenses clear, the memories flow,
In colors bright, the feelings glow.
Snapshots of laughter, tears, and glee,
In pictures of motion, we are free.

The dance of time, a fleeting glance,
Each image whispers its own chance.
From stillness born, the joy ignites,
In moments fleeting, our heart takes flight.

So let's create, let's paint the scene,
In frames of wonder, what might have been.
With each click, a journey starts,
Pictures in motion, etching our hearts.

In the Heart of the Expedition

With maps in hand and spirits high,
We set our course beneath the sky.
In every step, adventure calls,
To climb the peaks, to brave the falls.

The world unfolds, a tapestry bright,
In colors rich, a sheer delight.
Through forests deep, by rivers wide,
In the heart of the expedition, we glide.

Each path a story, each turn a chance,
In unity, we join the dance.
With open hearts, we seek the thrill,
In every moment, time stands still.

Through wild terrain, we find our way,
Chasing dreams, come what may.
In every heartbeat, the spirit's song,
In the heart of the expedition, we belong.

Fields of Glittering Grins

In the fields where daisies sway,
Children laugh and dance today.
Colors burst in vibrant play,
Shimmering dreams in bright display.

Sunlight kisses every face,
Joy and warmth in this embrace.
Whispers of a gentle breeze,
Spreading love among the trees.

A tapestry of colors bright,
Rays of gold in morning light.
Glittering smiles in every heart,
From this field, we never part.

In the evening's softening glow,
Memories of laughter flow.
Fields may fade, but never fear,
Their joy will always linger near.

A Celebration of the Soul

In the quiet of the night,
Stars are shining, pure delight.
Each a wish from deep within,
A celebration to begin.

With every heartbeat, let us sing,
Dance upon the joy we bring.
Spirit rising, pure and free,
Embracing all, camaraderie.

Moments shared, a sacred trust,
In the bond, we find our dust.
Life and love, they intertwine,
Together, hearts forever shine.

Grateful for this journey wide,
With companions by our side.
In the warmth of every cheer,
The essence of our souls is clear.

Chasing Joyful Echoes

In valleys bright where laughter rings,
We chase the joy that childhood brings.
Whispers of fun in the air,
Remind us all that we should care.

Footsteps light on paths of gold,
Joyful echoes, stories told.
Moments captured, hearts collide,
In the laughter, we confide.

Bright balloons against blue skies,
Hopes and dreams begin to rise.
Chasing echoes of delight,
In every laugh, the world feels right.

Together, through the hills we roam,
Finding joy, we feel at home.
In this chase, we lose all fears,
Chasing echoes, laughter cheers.

Adventures in Laughter

Let's embark on journeys wide,
With laughter as our joyful guide.
Through valleys deep, across the plains,
Every giggle, sweet refrains.

With friends beside, adventures bloom,
In every laugh, dispelling gloom.
Together we will climb each hill,
Chasing dreams that make us thrill.

Moments shared under the sun,
In this quest, we all have fun.
Laughter echoes through the air,
Adventures waiting everywhere.

As stars emerge and night draws near,
Our hearts are light, our path is clear.
In laughter's arms, we find our way,
Living fully, day by day.

Sunbeams and Streamers

Golden rays spill through trees,
Dancing shadows on the ground.
Whispers in the gentle breeze,
Nature's beauty, so profound.

Children laugh beneath the sun,
Running wild in fields so green.
Moments shared, hearts beat as one,
In this world, pure and serene.

Clouds drift slowly, paint the sky,
Colors blend, a soft embrace.
Time stands still as dreams can fly,
Memories linger in this space.

Evening comes, the sun dips low,
Stars awaken, twinkling bright.
As night descends, we still glow,
Guided by the moon's soft light.

The Odyssey of Radiance

Across the sea, the dawn ascends,
Waves of gold crash on the shore.
A journey starts, the light transcends,
Each moment cherished, wanting more.

Sails unfurl in morning's gleam,
Guided by an endless quest.
Adventure calls, it feels like a dream,
With every breath, we feel so blessed.

Mountains rise, the sun ignites,
Peaks adorned with colors bright.
Through valleys deep, in starry nights,
Radiance echoes, pure delight.

At journey's end, we stand as one,
Hearts alight, forever changed.
A tale of light, a life begun,
In this odyssey, we're now arranged.

Chasing Light

In the dawn, we start to race,
Chasing shadows, fleeting time.
Every moment, every place,
Guided by the sun's sweet rhyme.

Through the woods, where secrets hide,
Sunbeams dance on leaves so high.
In this magic, we confide,
As daylight whispers, 'Do not shy.'

Footsteps echo on the ground,
Each heartbeat quickens, takes its flight.
In the silence, joy is found,
Living boldly in the light.

As dusk arrives, the chase may end,
But memories will softly glow.
In every heart, the light transcends,
Forever dancing, ever so.

Adventures in Bliss

With open eyes, we roam the lands,
In every corner, joy appears.
Hand in hand, we make our plans,
Creating memories through the years.

Beneath the stars, we find our way,
Guided by laughter, love, and trust.
In every moment, we will stay,
In this adventure, we are just.

Mountains climbed and rivers crossed,
Every trial makes us grow strong.
In our hearts, there's not a loss,
Together, we will sing our song.

As sunsets paint the world in hues,
We bask in moments filled with bliss.
In every dream that we choose,
Life's adventure is a tender kiss.

Meadows of Merriment

In fields of gold where laughter sings,
The breeze whispers of joyful things.
Sunlight dances on petals bright,
A canvas of dreams in pure delight.

Children chase the butterflies,
With twinkling stars in their eyes.
Nature's laughter fills the air,
A symphony beyond compare.

Flowers sway in the gentle breeze,
Rustling softly like whispered pleas.
Each moment a treasure to behold,
In meadows where tales of joy are told.

Beneath the sky of endless blue,
Friendship blossoms, pure and true.
In this haven of simple cheer,
We dance through life, year after year.

Caravans of Elation

Beneath the vast and starlit skies,
Caravans roll where the spirit flies.
Laughter echoes through the night,
Every heart filled with delight.

With every journey, tales unfold,
Of courage, warmth, and dreams of gold.
Together we weave a story long,
In every note of our wandering song.

Paths intertwined, we roam and play,
Collecting moments along the way.
In elation, we find our place,
Embracing life's swift, gentle race.

The morning light calls us anew,
Painted horizons in vibrant hue.
Forever chasing the bright unknown,
In caravans, we find our home.

Wandering with Wonder

Through whispering woods, we find our way,
In daylight's arms, where shadows play.
Each step a dance, each glance a spark,
Wandering forth into the dark.

The world around, a canvas wide,
With every heartbeat, dreams collide.
Mountains high and rivers deep,
Into the unknown, we take a leap.

In moments still, we pause and breathe,
Nature's secrets, heartstrings weave.
With every pause, a lesson learned,
In the fire of curiosity, we burn.

Wandering forth, hand in hand,
We paint our dreams upon the land.
With wonder held in every gaze,
We journey on through endless days.

Chasing Dusks and Dawns

As daylight fades and colors blend,
We chase the dusks that softly send
Whispers of night, a soothing balm,
In twilight's glow, the world feels calm.

With every dawn, hope rises high,
A canvas brushed with hues of sky.
The sun awakens, and shadows flee,
In chasing light, we find our glee.

Moments fleeting, yet deeply felt,
In every heartbeat, dreams are dealt.
A dance of shadows and golden rays,
We gather joy in countless ways.

Chasing the beauty that life bestows,
Through dusks serene and dawns that glow.
In this rhythm of night and morn,
We find our peace, forever reborn.

Pathways of Elation

In fields of gold, we roam and play,
With laughter bright, we greet the day.
Hearts wide open, spirits soar,
Each step we take, we crave for more.

In vibrant hues, the world unfolds,
With every journey, a story told.
Together we find our truest selves,
In this grand tale, love swiftly dwells.

Whispers of Wanderlust

Beneath the stars, our dreams ignite,
Caught in the glow of the moon's soft light.
With every breeze, a new path calls,
In whispered tones, the wild enthralls.

Mountains high and valleys wide,
Invite us on this thrilling ride.
With open hearts, we venture forth,
In wanderlust, we feel our worth.

The Dance of Discovery

With every turn, we find delight,
In shadows cast by morning light.
Each corner holds a tale to share,
Awakening wonders everywhere.

As steps align in rhythmic grace,
We twirl through time and space.
Uncharted paths beneath our feet,
In discovery, our souls complete.

Footprints in the Sun

On golden sands, our journeys trace,
The warmth of sun, a sweet embrace.
With every footprint left behind,
A mark of joy, and dreams combined.

Through laughter, tears, and stories spun,
We weave our lives, each day begun.
In sunlight's glow, together we run,
Forever cherished, the footprints won.

Milton Keynes UK
Ingram Content Group UK Ltd.
UKHW051811101024
449294UK00007BA/57